# Medieval Villages

by Evelyn Coleman

illustrated by Stephen Castanza

Harcourt

ISBN 0-15-323125-4

Ordering Options

ISBN 0-15-325523-4 (Grade 2 Advanced-Level Collection)

ISBN 0-15-326975-8 (package of 5)

2 3 4 5 6 7 8 9 10   179   10 09 08 07 06 05 04 03 02

# Medieval Villages

by Evelyn Coleman
illustrated by Stephen Castanza

Orlando   Boston   Dallas   Chicago   San Diego

Visit *The Learning Site!*

www.harcourtschool.com

In the Middle Ages, most people in Europe lived in villages. These people were known as peasants. Most didn't own land. Instead, they paid rent to landowners who were called lords.

# Medieval Villages

by Evelyn Coleman
illustrated by Stephen Castanza

Orlando   Boston   Dallas   Chicago   San Diego

Visit *The Learning Site!*

**www.harcourtschool.com**

In the Middle Ages, most people in Europe lived in villages. These people were known as peasants. Most didn't own land. Instead, they paid rent to landowners who were called lords.

Only a few hundred peasants lived in each village.
Because of the small number, they could develop close
ties with each other. The peasants built houses made
of mud and straw. They often shared their houses with
their animals.

Most peasants worked on their farms together. The men used heavy plows. Teams of four to eight oxen pulled the plows. The peasants shared their animals and tools. Part of their crops had to be given to the lord.

*Peasants ate the freshest vegetables from their gardens.*

There was no grocery store in the village. The peasants planted and harvested their own food in small gardens. The main meal consisted of bread, milk, eggs, and beans. Peasants also ate cheese, cabbage, turnips, oatmeal cakes, and porridge. Villagers feasted on chicken, rabbit, squirrel, or pigs only at special celebrations.

The people of a village had to have their grain ground at the lord's mills. Villagers caught with their own small mills were punished. The lord also owned the ovens for baking bread.

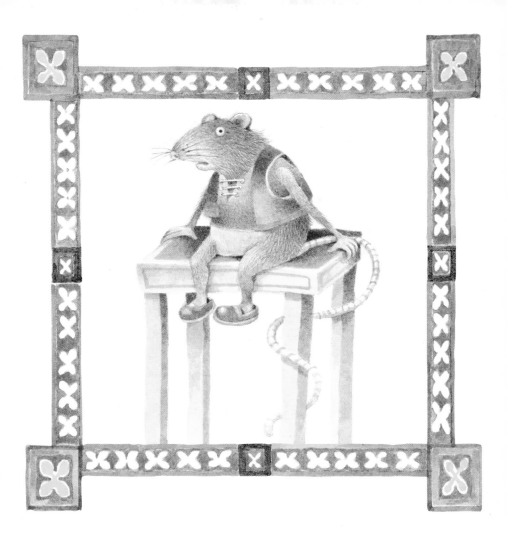

In the Middle Ages, the lords who owned the villages decided how people would be punished. People were not the only ones punished. Objects, such as swords, could be punished. Animals could be punished, too. Once a rat was put on trial.

There was no paper money during medieval times.
People used silver or gold coins. Villagers also bartered
with one another. That means they traded goods and
services for other goods and services. Villagers paid the
lord with work, money, or gifts.

*What is your name?*   *What be thy tide?*
*Where did you go?*    *Whereist did thy go?*
*What time is it?*     *How stands the hour?*

Villagers spoke English but not the English we speak in the United States today.

The women of a village shared many duties. They sheared sheep, wove wool, made quilts, cooked, and sometimes worked in the fields. Women also took care of the household and children. Women washed clothes together at a washing well.

Some villagers had special jobs. Blacksmiths shaped iron into farm tools for the village. A village herdsman took care of everyone's farm animals. Shoemakers and carpenters also worked in a village.

The Middle Ages were also known as the Dark
Ages because people did not have an interest in
learning. There were no schools or students sitting
at desks. Children worked hard with the adults.

Children tended a blacksmith's furious fire and fed the chickens early in the mornings. They pulled the ox to the next farmer, herded geese, and gathered feathers for beds. In free time, children made up games and played with homemade toys.

Villages had no doctors. They did have barber
surgeons, who cut hair and pulled teeth. To pull
a tooth, the barber surgeon strapped his patient to
a table. It looked a lot like an ironing board. Then
he yanked out the tooth. OUCH!

14

Living in a medieval village was not all work. There were many celebrations, such as May Day. On that day, graceful children danced around a Maypole.

15

Medieval villages vanished as more and more
people moved to towns. Today you can see medieval
life at fairs. These fairs are held all across the United
States. People dress up in costumes and do things that
were popular in medieval times.

# Think and Respond

1 What time in history does this story tell about?

2 What meats did the villagers eat at celebrations?

3 What did you learn about small communities by reading this story?

4 How do you know that people in medieval villages worked hard?

5 How was a barber surgeon different from a doctor today?

6 What job would you like to do in a medieval village?

 **Create a Game** Create a game you could have played in medieval times.

 **School-Home Connection** Is there a medieval fair near you? Find out.

**Word Count:** 584

ISBN 0-15-323125-4

90000>

9 780153 231254

Harcourt

# Medieval Villages

by Evelyn Coleman

illustrated by Stephen Castanza

Harcourt

# Medieval Villages

by Evelyn Coleman

illustrated by Stephen Castanza

Harcourt

ISBN 0-15-323125-4

Ordering Options

ISBN 0-15-325523-4 (Grade 2 Advanced-Level Collection)

ISBN 0-15-326975-8 (package of 5)

2 3 4 5 6 7 8 9 10   179   10 09 08 07 06 05 04 03 02

In the Middle Ages, most people in Europe lived in
villages. These people were known as peasants. Most
didn't own land. Instead, they paid rent to landowners
who were called lords.

2